EMORY ANDREW TA
MORODE

The Andrew Tate Method
*How to Get Rich, Get Women,
and Beat the Matrix*

EMORY ANDREW TATE

ALSO BY EZIO MORODER:

Get Her: A Step-By-Step Guide for Meeting, Dating, and Seducing Your Dream Girl

Do you want to stop being scared of going up to beautiful women and start seeing results? Use this guide to find your DREAM GIRL.

If you think you need to shell out thousands of dollars to get her, think again. This straightforward step-by-step guide for dating and seduction will teach you how to turn her from a stranger to a sexual partner (or even your girlfriend).

STEP 1: Do You Before You Do Her
will teach you how to harness your Unique Self, getting out of your own way and stopping overthinking in its tracks. It will also teach you ways to maximize your Confidence and Health while diving deep into Meditative techniques.
- Get Your Mind Right through Meditation, Reframing, Grounding, and more ego hacks
- Learn how to carry yourself with Confidence, Empathy, and a Sense of Humor
- Get Out of the House with key teachings on how to broaden your Social Circle and Networking

STEP 2: Go Up To Her (Or DM Her)
will teach you how to optimize your approach up to a beautiful woman, including how to recognize Signs of Interest from her. It will also delve into Online Dating Apps and give you a play-by-play on how to secure a date (or more...)
- learn how to Approach without Hesitation
- understand the dangers of Chasing Validation
- become a master in the art of Recognizing Signs of Interest

- harness the power of the dating apps by curating the perfect First Message

STEP 3: Ride the Wave (Conversation)
will outline how to Convey Value to the girl during the Conversation to set yourself up for success while standing out from the pack.
- get an endless list of ways to Convey Value, making you irresistible
- train to use Body Language to send her into a frenzy
- become a sex guru through the powerful act of Mirroring

STEP 4: Escalate and Elevate
tackles the process of Physical Escalation, Leading, and other need-to-knows that will have women desperate for you to take it further.
- discover how to Gain Compliance from the girl
- learn the powerful Bait/Hook/Reel/Release technique
- check out the different forms of Physical Escalation
- harness the power of Leading
- master online techniques including Conversation Threading

STEP 5: Always Be Closing
will teach you how to secure the close before it's happening with detailed sections on both Number Closing and Kiss Closing.
- Get her number with Direct and False Time Constraint number closing
- Get the kiss by using The Cheek Trick and other techniques
- Learn how to build online Rapport

STEP 6: Make Something Out of Nothing
guides you through setting up a date, from what and when to Text to picking the first date Venue.
- use texting techniques to get a surefire date
- how to pick the Venue and Time of the date
- how to Prepare for the date to get your mind and body ready

STEP 7: Turn a Date into a Seduction
will focus on what to say and do (and how to say and do it) while on the date, ultimately leading to how to finally Seduce her and get her into your bed (or hers.)

- show up to the date ready with powerful courting techniques
- master the art of Date Flirting
- maintain the "Us-and-Them Frame" to create an unbreakable bond
- learn how to get her back to your place
- uncover invaluable techniques to get her begging for sex

STEP 8: Keep Her
gives you the lowdown on how to make your dream girl into your girlfriend.

- how to handle the Morning After
- deciding if you're Compatible
- how to keep seducing her

The above only scratches the surface. This guide will have you set up for seduction and romantic mastery, giving you applicable knowledge and steps to use in order to get your Dream Girl!

CONTENTS

PREFACE

At the end of March, 2023, I walked out of a Romanian prison and smelled fresh air for the first time in months. You couldn't tell by looking at my face, but it was one of the best moments of my life. What you saw on the outside was a stone-cold fucking boss. You didn't see how I really felt because I didn't want you to.

The idiotic media and journalists were there for a snapshot of a big, mean criminal, and I was going to give them that. Their lives are pathetic anyway, while mine is amazing—might as well give them what they want and help them put food on the table before they inevitably lose their shitty job.

The face I showed the media that day was the face of a complete alpha. I didn't show how grateful I was to be out of prison, but I didn't need to. Those feelings were for me and me alone. And it wasn't a front, either. That hardened stare is my real face, earned through years of pushing through adversity.

I could easily complain about the fake news media running with a bullshit story, or I could complain about the Romanian authorities and their witch hunt, but I won't. The sad fact is that when you beat the matrix and live life as a true alpha male, saying what you want and exposing the lies to others, you get a big target on your back. Sometimes that target lands you in prison.

From early on, I have lived my life using a method of pure, unadulterated masculinity. This way of life has gotten me to heights never thought possible. I've gotten beautiful women, even more beautiful cars, and a financial empire that is unprecedented in its reach and impact. The simple fact is that you can do the same.

This book will give detailed insight into my methodical approach to living. It will shatter your preconceived notions of how to live in the world, and it will push you out of your comfort zone, forcing you to confront your bullshit head-on and negate it through sheer will.

You are fucking up left and right. Don't be ashamed of it or bitch and moan. Take your power back by living by a tried and true method that, while possibly putting a target on your back, will definitely end your insignificance and turn you into the man you are meant to be. I'm not special, I'm just focused and dedicated to living a life unencumbered by the bullshit limitations the matrix tries to force on everybody.

So buckle the fuck up, because you're about to change your life. All you need is the willpower, the drive, and this book. No more bullshit excuses. No more bitching and moaning. Light up that cigar and dive in.

THE MATRIX

The Matrix is the perfect word to describe the current world which is controlled by the powerful entities behind it. Everything you see or hear is manipulated by the matrix to keep you away from what's actually happening.

The Matrix makes you believe in things it wants you to believe in, so you'll do things that it wants you to do. As the victims, no matter how hard you try, you still suffer, stay poor, and be depressed.

People are dumber than ever. Everyone, you included, are being fed nonsense through your phones, TVs, and culture. Take s look at your phone right now. Even spend 5 minuted on your phone this second, then come back.

Were those 5 minutes at all productive? You probably saw some tits, some whiners crying about how "unfair" the world is, and videos of people being beaten up or hurting themselves. Either that, or you ended up jacking off. Real productive, right? WRONG!

Look around you, for Christ's sake. What was once an incredible world filled with alpha males building great things is now a cesspool. The entire economy is based around idiots investing their time, energy, and money into trivial bullshit. The people in control want it that way.
They want you stupid and complacent. They want you weak-willed and helpless. That way, you can keep funneling your money to them in the naive hope that your life will get better. Newsflash,

fuckwad: It won't. You are wasting your life.

The fake-ass news media holds immense power in shaping how you feel and what you do. The concentration of media ownership and control has led to biased reporting and the manipulation of information. In many instances, media outlets are influenced by political and corporate interests, leading to the distortion of facts and the promotion of specific agendas. These agendas are almost always based upon killing man's will to exert power in an attempt to turn all of you into beta sheep.

Sensationalism and clickbait culture further dumb down everyone, all the time. News organizations, driven by the need for higher ratings and online engagement, prioritize attention-grabbing headlines over nuanced or factual reporting. This results in the spread of misinformation and the creation of a polarized environment where complex issues are oversimplified and the average person is turned into a mouth-breathing idiot.

Listen, I fucking love social media. I built my empire on it. But that is because I know what I'm doing, and I use social media to my advantage. Almost nobody else does. Most of you are slaves to social media, not conquerors like me.

The advent of social media has transformed how information is disseminated, creating echo chambers where individuals are exposed primarily to content that aligns with their existing beliefs (most of which are already stupid and hurting your chances at success). Algorithms on platforms like Facebook and Instagram are designed to reinforce users' preferences, creating a feedback loop that limits exposure to diverse perspectives, which means you are stuck in your own little beta world of loserdom.

Moreover, social media platforms are increasingly being exploited for disinformation campaigns. Foreign actors, political entities, and interest groups utilize targeted messaging and manipulation tactics to sow discord, exploit societal fault lines, and influence public opinion. The rapid spread of misinformation through these channels makes it challenging for the idiot masses to discern fact from fiction.

The above is why the world immediately thought I was guilty of a heinous crime when it was patently obvious that I was innocent. The media and echo chambers had their "facts," and everyone went along with it because everyone is trapped in the matrix.

But not me. I'm out of prison, totally exonerated, and still living life as a true alpha male who doesn't give a fuck. And you can, too.

I have been a sad man and a stupid slave in my early life, but I found the way out. The Matrix is now cracked, there is a proven way to get what you truly want in life. That proven way is by following the methods outlined in this book.

Don't be arrogant and think that you can do it yourself. Look at you in the mirror, are you really fine? If the answer is no, well, it's actually GOOD. You realized it, while thousands of "superheroes" have not.

The clock is ticking my friends, and it's not going to stop. So, stop being lazy, arrogant, and procrastinating like the losers around you that are completely controlled by the matrix and its manipulative information.

FROM NOTHING TO KING

EVERY JOURNEY HAS A BEGINNING

Let me tell you more about how fed up I am with the world right now. Men are turning into broke, wimpy, weak, virtue-signaling pussies. The matrix mindset has everyone so wrapped up in a bubble that they can't see how pathetic they've become. So, I've taken it upon myself to show you nothings how to become somethings: a genuine man, an alpha male. Allow me to share a bit of my history.

I was born into a life filled with challenges. My old man, Emory Andrew Tate II, was a chess Grandmaster and a kickboxing world champion. So, you could say I was bred for greatness. But it wasn't all sunshine and rainbows, my friends. I faced racism, poverty, and all sorts of challenges that would break a lesser man. But the thing is – I ain't no lesser man. I confronted those challenges, learned from them, and turned them into the fire that fuels me every damn day.

You see, being an alpha male isn't just about having muscles or scoring with hot chicks (although, believe me, that's a damn sweet perk). It's about transcending the mediocrity society expects from you. It's about taking charge of your life and destiny, not being a damn sheep. So, why is it crucial to be an alpha male?

Well, for starters, you'll earn the respect of your peers, and that's something money can't buy. You'll wield the power to influence and lead others, and let me tell you, there's no better feeling than being in control. You'll become the type of man other men look up to, and the kind of man that women admire.

You might be thinking this all sounds fantastic, but you're likely also pondering, "Tate, how the hell do I actually become an alpha male?" Well, my friends, that's precisely what this book is about. I'm giving you the blueprint to metamorphose from a weak-ass excuse for a man into a genuine alpha male. Throughout these pages, I'll be dishing out stories from my own life – the good, the bad, and the ugly. I've been through it all and emerged on the other side stronger, smarter, and more successful than ever. And guess what? You can too.

We'll delve into everything from cultivating a resilient mindset to throwing punches like a true man. We'll discuss leadership, relationships, and all the elements that define an alpha male. By the time you finish this book, you'll possess the tools and knowledge to become the man you've always aspired to be. But let me caution you – this journey won't be a cakewalk. It's going to demand blood, sweat, and tears. You'll need to confront your demons, tackle your weaknesses, and push through your limits. But I assure you, it'll be damn well worth it. So strap in, motherfuckers, because it's time to embrace the alpha male you were destined to become.

Now, before we plunge into the details, let me set some ground rules. This book isn't for pussy-boys who are easily offended or those who can't handle hard truths. If you can't handle it, then this ain't the book for you. So, assuming you're still with me, I reckon you're ready to roll up your sleeves and evolve into the badass alpha male you're destined to become.

Let me make something crystal clear – nobody is born an alpha male. It's not some innate trait you either have or don't have. Being an alpha male is a damn choice. It's a decision you make every day to rise above, be stronger, and smarter than the weak betas around you. If you're up for the challenge, you can become an alpha male, regardless of your background or who you are. One of the initial steps is taking a good, hard look in the mirror and being brutally honest with yourself. Identify your weaknesses, confront your fears, and recognize what's holding you back. You can't fix what you don't acknowledge, so own your stuff and be ready to confront it head-on.

After that, start building a solid foundation for your new alpha male life. Get your body in top-notch shape, learn self-defense, and cultivate the mental resilience to tackle any challenge. Trust me, there's nothing like the confidence of knowing you can handle any situation, whether it's a street brawl or a high-stakes negotiation. However, being an alpha male isn't just about being tough. It's about comprehending the world around you and mastering the art of navigating it to your advantage.

Become a maestro of social dynamics, understand what makes people tick, and learn how to influence them. Master the art of seduction, not just for casual encounters (though, once again, a nice perk), but to build influential relationships that will propel you to greater heights.

In this book, I'm laying bare the lessons learned through a rollercoaster of life experiences—ups and downs, triumphs and failures, victories and defeats. I'll spill the beans on how I crafted a multi-million dollar business empire, rose to the ranks of a world-class kickboxer, and navigated the tricky waters of the dating scene. Get ready for the inside scoop on the tactics and strategies that propelled me above the competition, shaping the man I am today. But don't expect me to sugarcoat it or offer a comforting hand. I'm serving it straight, no chaser.

There's no room for excuses or self-pity in the alpha male world. Success demands a willingness to do whatever it takes, even if it means getting a bit dirty and stepping on a few toes along the way. So, are you ready for the ride of a lifetime? Are you prepared to put in the work and evolve into the best version of yourself? Ready to claim your spot among the true alpha males?

If the answer is yes, then let's get fucking started, no holds barred.

MASCULINITY AND BEING ALPHA

Listen up, you sorry fuckin soy-boy whiners. It's high time to confront the reality: society has turned men into betas. We're stuck in a world brimming with mediocrity-loving pussies who never strive for their full potential. But that's not your deal, right? You're here because you aspire to be a bona fide alpha male – the type who couldn't care less about others' opinions.

So, what's the deal with being an alpha male? Some folks think it's all about being a jerk to everyone, but that's not the whole picture. Being an alpha male is about being a leader, a warrior, and a man who takes control of his own life. It's about standing tall in the face of adversity and never caving in. It's about being the kind of man that earns the respect of other men and catches the eye of women.

First things first, grasp that masculinity isn't some outdated notion to toss aside. Sure, there are dudes who use it as an excuse to be jerks, but that's not the essence of true masculinity. Genuine masculinity is about strength, honor, and integrity. It's about being a shield and a provider. It's about embracing your role as a man without hesitation. Now, I know what's running through your mind: "But Tate, isn't that some old-fashioned idea of what a man should be?"

Hell no. Just take a look around – the world is crawling with feeble, miserable men clueless about who they are or what they're capable of. They're prisoners to the matrix mindset, merely going through the motions and never seizing control of their lives. That's not the kind of man you aim to be, is it?

So, how do you turn into an alpha male who couldn't care less about the bullshit society tries to shovel down your throat? It all kicks off with your mindset. Trash all that miserable self-doubt and insecurity that's been dragging you down. Start believing in yourself and your ability to kick any obstacle's ass that dares cross your path. It's about having the mental strength to stare down your fears and grind them into the dirt with your boot.

But it's not just about being tough. An alpha male stands firm on his principles, period. He knows what the hell he stands for and won't back down, no matter the cost. He's not swayed by others' opinions because he gets that true power comes from deep inside. In this book, I'm laying out the roadmap to become that kinda guy – the one who couldn't give a damn about what others think.

We'll dive deep into masculinity, leadership, and throwing punches, and I'll spill my own tales as a four-time kickboxing world champion and badass entrepreneur. But fair warning: this journey ain't for the weak-hearted. You're gonna have to stare down some brutal truths about yourself and the messed-up world around you. You're gonna have to push yourself harder than you ever thought possible. But if you're up for the damn challenge, I swear one thing: you'll come out the other side as a true alpha male who doesn't give a single damn. And believe me, there's no better feeling in the world.

THE ALPHA MALE MENTALITY
THE INNER ALPHA

Alright, so you've made the decision to become an alpha male who doesn't give a fuck. Good on you. But that means you've got to kick off by boosting your confidence, self-assurance, resilience, and charisma. These are the qualities that'll separate you from the rest of the herd and empower you to seize control of your life.

Let's kick things off with confidence. It's the foundation upon which everything else is built. Without it, you'll never tackle your fears, take risks, or stand your ground. Now, the issue is, most guys have no clue how to beef up their confidence. They think it's some innate thing you either have or don't. But that's nonsense. Confidence can be developed, just like any other damn skill.

So, how do you build your confidence? Step one is to stop caring about what other people think. Most guys are so anxious about judgment or rejection that they never take risks or put themselves out there. That's not how an alpha male rolls. An alpha male knows the only opinion that truly matters is his own. So, quit stressing about what others think and focus on what the hell you want.

Next up, you've got to start taking action. Confidence isn't something you can just think your way into – you've got to prove to yourself that you can conquer obstacles and reach your goals. Set small, achievable targets and work your way up. Every damn time you succeed, your confidence will shoot up. And even when you fail, you'll learn damn valuable lessons that'll toughen you up and make you more resilient.

Now, let's delve into the realm of self-assurance. This quality revolves around recognizing your worth and feeling at ease with your true self. It's about embracing both your strengths and weaknesses and not allowing others to dictate your identity. To cultivate self-assurance, delve deeper into self-discovery. Take some time to reflect on your values, goals, and passions. Don't be a girl about it-really think hard without letting emotions overtake you. Once you have a clear understanding of your identity and principles, projecting self-assurance to the world becomes a whole lot easier.

Resilience stands out as another pivotal trait for any alpha male. Life throws challenges and setbacks our way, but an alpha male doesn't let that derail him. Instead, he learns from mistakes and persists, no matter how challenging the circumstances. To foster resilience, start welcoming adversity. Cease avoiding challenges and confront them head-on. The more you confront such situations, the more robust and resilient you'll become.

Lastly, let's touch on charisma. Charisma is the secret ingredient that draws people to follow, listen, and want to be around you. It's a blend of confidence, charm, and genuine interest in others. To nurture charisma, focus on honing your communication skills. Learn to be an attentive listener, pose engaging questions, and make people feel valued and appreciated. Simultaneously, practice assertiveness in expressing your own opinions and ideas. Striking a balance between these two aspects propels you well on your path to becoming a charismatic leader of both men and, more importantly, women.

But the chapter ain't over yet, so learn the above and fucking strap in.

ALPHA BODY LANGUAGE
AND COMMUNICATION

Alright, you've nailed down your confidence, self-assurance, resilience, and charisma. Now, let's shift our focus to another vital element of being an alpha male: mastering the intricacies of communication and body language. Why is this a big deal? Because communication is the linchpin for building robust relationships, influencing people, and securing what you want in life. And a significant chunk of that revolves around body language.

First off, let's tackle verbal communication. As an alpha male, your ability to express yourself clearly and assertively is crucial. This means being straightforward, concise, and straight to the point. No beating around the bush or sugarcoating – people appreciate honesty, even if it's a tad harsh. And never shy away from standing up for yourself and your opinions. Remember, an alpha male couldn't care less about others' dumbfuck opinions.

However, communication isn't solely about talking – it's equally about listening. Many idiot guys make the blunder of dominating conversations, leaving no room for others to voice their thoughts. That's not how an alpha male rolls. A genuine alpha male understands the importance of active listening and engaging with others. He poses questions, demonstrates sincere interest, and ensures people feel heard and understood.

Now, let's delve into body language. Your non-verbal cues convey a wealth of information about your identity and emotions, even when you're not uttering a word. As an alpha male, it's imperative to be mindful of the signals you're sending and ensure they align with the image you aim to project.

Your posture: it fucking sucks and you know it. Stand tall,

shoulders back, and chest out. Not only does this make you appear more confident and powerful, but it also contributes to how you feel. Maintain eye contact when you're in a conversation – it indicates your engagement and interest without going overboard into creepy, staring-like-a-psycho territory.

Moving on to another crucial aspect of body language – facial expressions. Master the art of controlling your emotions to project the desired image. If you're aiming for a friendly and approachable vibe, throw in a smile and maintain a relaxed expression. For a more dominant and assertive aura, keep your face neutral with a strong gaze. Gestures matter too. Let your hands and arms emphasize your points and convey your feelings. Just steer clear of going overboard – wild arm flailing only makes you look ridiculous. Keep your movements deliberate and controlled.

Lastly, stay mindful of others' body language. Tune in to the subtle cues people emit and adjust your approach accordingly. If someone appears uneasy or defensive, ease the tension by matching their body language and mirroring their movements. On the flip side, if they're open and engaged, feel free to assert yourself and take control of the conversation.

In this chapter, we've explored the significance of mastering the art of communication and body language for the alpha male who doesn't give a fuck. By refining your verbal and non-verbal communication skills, you'll wield the power to influence people, cultivate impactful relationships, and command respect from those in your orbit.

Remember, though, that becoming a master of communication and body language takes time and practice. You're not going to become a smooth-talking, body language-reading machine overnight. But with dedication and effort, you'll be well on your way to becoming the kind of alpha male who doesn't give a lousy fuck and can navigate any social situation with ease.

STRENGTH
HEALTH AND IMAGE

You're a lazy fuck and you know it. It's time to face the facts about physical fitness, strength, and self-defense. This goes beyond merely admiring yourself in the mirror, although that's a pleasant side effect. It's about embodying a robust, capable man who can safeguard himself and those he values. So, let's dig in.First and foremost, you've got to keep yourself in shape. I'm not talking about some pansy-ass lightweight cardio routine where you jog on the treadmill for 20 minutes and call it quits. I'm talking about a hardcore, full-body workout that'll push you to your limits and make you feel like you're on the brink of collapse. Why? Because that's the price of being an alpha male.

Now, I know what's running through your mind: "Tate, I don't have hours to dedicate to working out every day." Well, surprise, neither do I. But I still carve out the time to hit the gym and train like a beast. Why? Because it's a damn priority. To be a genuine alpha male, you've got to make fitness a non-negotiable part of your life. And don't even get me started on diet. If you're loading up on processed junk and washing it down with soda, forget about achieving the body you desire. You need to fuel yourself with clean, whole foods – lean meats, vegetables, and healthy fats. Cut out the sugar and processed trash, and witness your body undergo a transformation.

But maintaining physical fitness isn't just about aesthetic appeal – it's about cultivating strength and power. This is why it's crucial to lift heavy weights and concentrate on compound exercises like squats, deadlifts, and bench presses. These workouts are the key to building substantial muscle and unleashing a feeling of superhero strength.

Now, let's transition to the superhero realm and delve into self-defense. Being an alpha male who couldn't care less loses its point if you can't safeguard yourself or those close to you. That's why it's imperative to acquire skills in martial arts or combat sports – be it boxing, Muay Thai, Brazilian Jiu-Jitsu, or any other discipline.

I understand your reservations: "But Tate, I don't want to take punches or get choked out." Tough shit. Life is challenging, and to be a genuine alpha male, you must be equipped to handle adversity. Moreover, there's nothing more invigorating than stepping into the ring or onto the mats and testing your abilities against another human being.

So, how do you kick off this journey? It's straightforward: locate a gym or martial arts school in your vicinity and enroll in classes. Don't fret about being the least experienced or weakest person in the room – everyone starts somewhere. Just show up, put in the effort, and maintain consistency. Over time, you'll witness progress, and your confidence will soar.

In summary, if you aspire to be an alpha male indifferent to the opinions of others, prioritize physical fitness, strength, and self-defense. Maintaining good physical shape is not only about aesthetics but is crucial for developing the mental toughness and discipline essential for true alpha males. Learning the art of self-defense is a fundamental skill for any man aiming to protect himself and his loved ones.

So, what's holding you back? Enough with the bullshit excuses – it's time to take action. Head to the gym, clean up your diet, and start mastering those punches or submissions. Remember, embodying the spirit of an alpha male who doesn't give a fuck involves more than just talking the talk – you've got to walk the walk.

And let me share a truth with you: the journey is immensely rewarding. There's nothing more gratifying than gazing in the mirror and witnessing the physical manifestation of your hard work and discipline in the form of a perfect specimen. When you can stand up for yourself and protect your loved ones, you'll truly embrace the essence of becoming an alpha male who couldn't care less.

So, quit reading this and start making moves. The sooner you commence, the sooner you'll reap the fruits of your labor. Believe me, once you start witnessing the results, you'll never want to revert to that weak, pathetic version of yourself.

Now, go out there and illustrate to the world what it means to be an alpha male who couldn't care less. And remember: no matter how tough it gets, no matter the pain, keep forging ahead. Genuine alpha males rise to challenges and conquer them, defying the odds.

I have faith in you, and I know you can pull this off. Go do it.

SELF-DEFENSE

Alright, pussies, it's time to elevate your skills and grasp the art of self-defense for both yourself and those you hold dear. Any alpha male worth their mettle won't stand idly by while someone threatens harm to themselves or their loved ones. So, let's delve into the realm of self-defense techniques and acquire some tangible skills.

First and foremost, seek out a martial art or combat sport that aligns with your personality and interests. There's no universal solution here – some may be drawn to the striking techniques of boxing or Muay Thai, while others might prefer the grappling and submission skills of Brazilian Jiu-Jitsu or wrestling. The key is to discover something you're passionate about, as that passion will be the driving force to keep you motivated and dedicated.

Now, I'm not suggesting you become the next Bruce Lee or Conor McGregor. However, you do need to attain proficiency to handle yourself in a physical altercation. This entails investing time and learning from the best. Locate a reputable gym or martial arts school and commit to consistent training. Remember, just like Rome wasn't built in a day, neither are formidable fighters.

In the realm of self-defense, one of the paramount aspects is situational awareness. Continuously scan your surroundings, identifying potential threats or dangers. The most effective way to defend yourself is to steer clear of a confrontation altogether. Trust your instincts, and stay attuned to your environment – often, they provide early warning signs crucial for ensuring your safety.

However, despite your best efforts, there may be occasions when you find yourself in a situation where you have to engage physically. When that occurs, you must be prepared to

EMORY ANDREW TATE

take decisive action. This involves understanding how to strike effectively, execute takedowns, and escape from unfavorable positions. Equally important is possessing the mental resilience to remain composed and focused under pressure – panicking will only expose you to harm and make you look weak.

Let's shift our focus to defending others. Being an alpha male who doesn't give a fuck isn't solely about self-preservation – it extends to safeguarding those you hold dear. Whether it's your family, friends, or your significant other, you must be ready and willing to step forward and shield them if a challenging situation arises.

This entails being vigilant about their safety, intervening if you perceive them in jeopardy, and being willing to put yourself in harm's way for their sake. True alpha males don't shy away or seek refuge when confronted with difficulties; instead, they confront the danger head-on and address it, regardless of the consequences.

In summary, acquiring self-defense skills and the ability to protect both yourself and others is a vital aspect of embodying the essence of an alpha male who couldn't care less. It's about being robust, proficient, and self-assured in your capabilities – and utilizing those capabilities to safeguard the well-being of those you care about. So, select a martial art or combat sport that resonates with you and commence training like a warrior.

Keep in mind: the path to becoming a genuine alpha male is arduous and prolonged. However, it's worthwhile – knowing you possess the skills and courage to confront and combat challenges when it truly matters is an unparalleled feeling.

Now, go out there and exemplify what it means to be an alpha male who couldn't care less. Train rigorously, maintain focus, and never shy away from a challenge. To provide a touch of inspiration, let me share some tales from my own kickboxing career.

During my earlier years as a determined and aspiring fighter, I ventured into a tournament that far exceeded my skill level. The competition included individuals who had been honing their craft for years, and I was well aware that I was in for a challenging experience. However, rather than retreating or succumbing to self-doubt, I made the decision to wholeheartedly embrace the challenge – because that's what true alpha males do.

In my first match, I faced an opponent with a formidable reputation for knocking people out. Stepping into the ring, I locked eyes with him and thought, "Fuck it, let's go." The bell rang, and we engaged in a fierce, primal exchange. Despite absorbing some powerful blows, I relentlessly pressed forward, utterly refusing to concede. Ultimately, I delivered a devastating combination that sent him crashing to the canvas.

This triumph imparted a valuable lesson: confronting your fears and taking on formidable opponents can lead to extraordinary achievements. This principle has remained a guiding force throughout my entire career, both within and beyond the confines of the ring.

Another standout moment from my kickboxing journey occurred during a championship title bout. Recognizing the high stakes, I understood that I couldn't afford any errors. Consequently, I trained with an unwavering intensity, pushing my physical and mental capacities to their absolute limits.

Entering the ring on the night of the fight, I felt invincible. Despite facing a skilled opponent, I was confident in my exhaustive preparations for this pivotal moment. The match unfolded as a grueling, back-and-forth struggle, with both of us investing everything we had.

In the climactic final round, I tapped into an unexpected reservoir of strength. Unleashing a barrage of punches and kicks, I overwhelmed my opponent, securing not only the victory but also the coveted championship belt.

The moments I've lived through in my kickboxing journey have played a significant role in molding the person I am today. They are a crucial factor in why I am so fervently dedicated to imparting the significance of physical fitness, strength, and self-defense to others. Having personally experienced the demands of confronting fears, overcoming challenges, and achieving triumph, I am driven to share these lessons.

Allow these narratives to ignite inspiration within you, motivating you to evolve into the finest version of yourself – an alpha male who remains indifferent to setbacks, who doesn't give a fuck. Embrace the trials, persevere through the hardships, and steadfastly pursue your path to greatness, never relenting in your pursuit.

DRESS FOR SUCCESS
ALPHA WARDROBE

Listen up, you fashion-challenged motherfuckers: it's time to elevate your style and curate a wardrobe that mirrors your alpha male status. I'm not suggesting you transform into a runway model or empty your wallet on designer labels, but you do need to be mindful of your appearance and ensure you're projecting the right image to the world.

First and foremost, invest in some top-notch, well-fitting garments. There's nothing worse than some idiot strolling around in a baggy, poorly-fitting suit or jeans that are a couple of sizes too large. While you don't have to splurge excessively, be willing to spend a bit more for clothes that not only fit you perfectly but are also crafted from quality materials.

Now, let's delve into the essentials. Every alpha male's wardrobe should include a few key items:

A killer suit: A finely tailored suit is indispensable for any alpha male. You never know when you'll need to attend a business meeting or a sophisticated event, so make sure you're always looking your best. Invest in at least one high-quality suit that complements your physique.

A badass leather jacket: It doesn't matter who you are – a leather jacket adds a cool factor to any ensemble. This timeless piece brings an edge to your look, making you resemble a genuine rockstar.

High-quality denim: A fantastic pair of jeans is a fundamental component of any alpha male's wardrobe. Identify a brand and fit that suits your body type, and don't hesitate to spend a bit more for a pair that promises durability.

Fashionable, adaptable footwear: You don't need an overflowing shoe collection, but having a few reliable pairs for various occasions is essential. Acquire classic, impeccably crafted dress shoes for formal events, a stylish pair of sneakers for casual outings, and some boots for those times when you need to assert yourself.

Statement-making accessories: Elevate your outfit with a tasteful watch, a standout pair of sunglasses, and a selection of carefully chosen accessories. Exercise moderation, but select pieces that showcase your personality and make a lasting impression.

Now that you've covered the fundamentals, it's time to cultivate your personal style – an opportunity to let your inner alpha male shine. Whether you're a rugged biker enthusiast who revels in leather and chains or a polished, sophisticated gentleman who favors tailored suits and designer labels, own your vibe and wear it with confidence.

A significant aspect of developing your personal style involves experimenting with diverse looks and discovering what resonates with you. Embrace risks and new experiences – that's how you'll uncover your authentic style and master the art of rocking it like a fucking boss.

Lastly, bear in mind that your appearance is just one facet of the equation. Being an alpha male is more than skin deep; it's about feeling good as well. Ensure you're tending to your body, staying in shape, and adopting a healthy lifestyle. Because when you exude the confidence of a million bucks, you'll undoubtedly look the part too.

Crafting an alpha male wardrobe revolves around selecting high-quality, well-fitting attire that mirrors your personal style and resonates with the badass within. Invest in the essentials, take style risks, and confidently own your look. And always remember: embodying the essence of an alpha male who doesn't give a fuck involves not just dressing the part but living it too.

Allow me to share a personal anecdote to illustrate. In the early stages of establishing my sterling reputation, I recognized the significance of my appearance. People form judgments based on looks, and I refused to be perceived as just another ordinary dumbfuck guy. So, I embraced dressing like the alpha male I knew I embodied – and the impact was profound.

Stepping into a room adorned in a meticulously tailored suit or sporting my favored leather jacket caught people's attention. I could sense the respect in their eyes, and the focus shifted to me. Dressing like an alpha male possesses the potency to command respect and distinguish you from the crowd.

Yet, it wasn't solely about the clothing. I prioritized physical self-care – exercising, eating well, and maintaining optimal fitness. Looking good translates to feeling good, and when you exude confidence and power, it becomes palpable.

To evolve into an alpha male, start by upgrading your wardrobe and refining your personal style. Invest in top-notch attire that not only fits impeccably but also resonates with the inner badass in you. Embrace diverse looks, take style risks, and assertively own your unique flair.

However, keep in mind the broader perspective. Being an alpha male extends beyond mere attire; it encompasses living the part as well. Ensure you tend to your body, stay in shape, and adopt a health-conscious lifestyle. When you exude the aura of looking and feeling exceptional, the world will reciprocate with the treatment you deserve.

Now, venture out there and exemplify what it truly means to be an alpha male. Make a bold statement through your style, embrace your confidence, and refuse to let anyone undermine your potential for greatness. Dress for success, live authentically, and take what's fucking yours.

ALPHA GROOMING

Pay attention, fucktards. Let's delve into a topic often overlooked by many but utterly vital for embodying an alpha male: grooming and personal style. Even if you boast the most exquisite wardrobe globally, sporting a scruffy beard, greasy locks, and bad breath will still make you look like a complete loser.

Beginning with the fundamentals – hygiene. It might sound obvious, yet it's astonishing how many guys overlook the straightforward acts of showering and brushing their teeth. If you aim to be an alpha male, commence by taking care of yourself and maintaining cleanliness. No one respects a man emitting unpleasant odors or appearing as though he just emerged from a dumpster. If you smell like shit, you are shit.

Having covered the basics, let's delve into grooming, the realm where true transformation occurs, setting alpha males apart from the rest. Attend to your hair, beard (if applicable), and skin. Regular haircuts, beard trims, and, for fuck's sake, facial moisturizing are essential. Trust me, it makes a significant difference.

Concerning hair, discover a style that suits you and stick to it. This doesn't mean you can't switch things up, but having a signature look reflecting your personality and alpha male status is crucial. If you're uncertain where to begin, seek advice from a skilled barber or hairstylist – they'll provide valuable guidance.

The realm of person style extends beyond your clothing – it's about your overall presentation to the world. It's reflected in your walk, your talk, and your overall demeanor. An alpha male, indifferent to the opinions of others, exudes confidence, self-assurance, and control. He's clear about his desires and unafraid to pursue them. He doesn't give a fuck.

Being an alpha doesn't require arrogance, but it demands standing firm for your beliefs. When faced with a challenge, don't retreat – hold your ground and assert your dominance. If you witness someone being disrespected, intervene and defend them. This is the conduct of a genuine alpha male.

In my personal life, I've consistently prioritized maintaining my appearance and projecting confidence. I understand that when I enter a room, people will judge me based on my appearance – and I want them to perceive me as the unequivocal boss that I am. Needless to say, they do.

To sum it up, embodying the essence of an alpha male goes beyond dressing well and having a stellar wardrobe. It involves self-care, proper grooming, and presenting yourself with confidence and swagger. If you aim to command respect and emerge as a true leader, every facet of your appearance and personal style requires attention.

Now, go out there promptly and illustrate to the world what it truly means to be an alpha male who disregards others' opinions. Be bold, be confident, and never allow anyone to convince you that achieving greatness is beyond your reach. Because when you exude the look and feel of a million bucks, you become unstoppable in making that million bucks.

FINANCIAL AND CAREER MASTERY
CULTIVATE THE SKILLS

Alright, dickwads, let's get straight to the point and dive into the essentials. If you're aiming to be an alpha, then you absolutely need to nurture discipline, ambition, and leadership skills that will elevate you to the pinnacle of success. I'm here to guide you through the process, so fasten your seatbelts, pay attention, and stop your fucking bitching.

Beginning with discipline, let's debunk any illusions or bullshit. Success doesn't simply drop into your lap; it demands hard work, unwavering dedication, and the fortitude to persist through challenges even when every part of you screams to give up. Make no mistake, without discipline, you're not going to thrive in this world. You'll merely be another individual struggling, dwelling in his mom's basement, lamenting the perceived unfairness of life while you masturbate like a dolt.

How do you cultivate discipline? Simple—set goals and adhere to them relentlessly. Aspiring to get in shape? Hit the gym every day. Dreaming of building a business? Clock in the hours and make it a reality. No excuses, no nonsense. This is the stark contrast distinguishing winners from losers.

Now, onto ambition. Do you think I reached my current position by lounging around, content with mediocrity? Absolutely not. I continually challenge myself to achieve more, to enhance, and to conquer fresh obstacles. That's precisely what you need to embody if you aspire to be anything more than a beta-bitch.

I've witnessed countless weak individuals with great potential squander their lives because they're hesitant to aim for big dreams. The fear of failure, rejection, or appearing foolish holds them back. Let me make one thing clear – the only truly foolish choice is leading a life brimming with remorse because you lacked the courage to pursue what you genuinely desired.

Lastly, let's delve into leadership. Aspiring to be an alpha male? Then, you must be a leader. Assume control, make decisions, and command respect. However, it also involves being a mentor, a role model, and someone willing to support others in their success.

Throughout my life, I've consistently embraced leadership roles, whether in kickboxing, business, or personal relationships. I've never shied away from taking charge or making difficult decisions. And you know what? People respect that. They follow because they trust I'll guide them to success, and I have time and time again.

So, for all you wanna-be alpha males, it's time to elevate your game. Develop discipline, ambition, and leadership skills, and witness the transformation of your life. Cease being a bitching pussy stuck in a cycle of hardship, and become a triumphant individual who seizes what they desire.

Remember, life doesn't reward the feeble, the hesitant, or the indolent. It rewards those who are audacious, resolute, and relentless in their pursuit of greatness. So, are you choosing to be a loser, or will you be an alpha male who doesn't give a fuck? The decision is yours.

BUILDING WEALTH

Alright, you peasants, let's address a topic that many shy away from: money. If you want to be an alpha male who doesn't give a fuck, then building wealth and achieving financial independence should be your focus. There's no space for financially struggling individuals in this lifestyle, so pay attention and take some notes. To truly not give a fuck, you need "fuck you" money.

First and foremost, understand this: money is power. It provides the freedom to do what you want, when you want, and with whom you want. I didn't reach my current status by being broke and pathetic. No, I constructed my empire and continue to expand it daily.

So, how do you accumulate wealth? It begins with having a well-thought-out plan and a work ethic that outshines everyone else. Being lazy won't cut it if you expect to make money – it simply doesn't work that way. You have to hustle, grind, and dedicate the hours needed to turn your dreams into reality.

Next, you must invest. Do you think I amassed my wealth by stashing money in a savings account? Hell no. I invested in businesses, real estate, stocks, and more. And you know what? It paid off. Educate yourself about various investment strategies and choose the ones that suit you. The crucial factor is to diversify your portfolio, allowing your money to work for you while you're catching some Zs (but not as many hours as the rest of the idiots sleep).

Financial independence isn't just about having a shit-ton of money in the vault – it's about being able to live life on your terms without worrying about how you're going to get by. You want to travel the world? Go for it. You want to buy a fucking Lambo? Do it. Decide what you want nd go for it without any hesitation.

But let me tell you, achieving financial independence isn't handed to you on a silver platter. You've got to put in the work and be disciplined with your money. That involves living within your means, consistently saving and investing, and always keeping an eye out for new opportunities to grow your wealth.

And seriously, don't be one of those fucking idiots who squanders all their money on frivolous things like designer clothes and overpriced bottles at the club. That's a guaranteed route to ending up broke and miserable. Instead, invest in yourself and your future. Use your money on things that contribute to your personal growth as an individual and as an alpha male.

Here's a little secret for you: the truly wealthy don't give a shit about what others think of them. They don't feel the need to prove anything because they understand their own value. They don't waste time trying to impress people with their money – they simply live life to the fullest and relish the rewards of their hard work.

So, if you're aiming to be an alpha male, it's time to embark on the journey of building wealth and attaining financial independence. Get moving, put in the effort, make smart investments, and live life on your own terms. The world is ripe for the taking – will you seize it, or will you let it slip away like a beta bitch?

The choice is yours, gentlemen. Make it count.

GET RICH
DROPSHIPPING FOR DUMMIES

If you're a poor loser, there is abso-fucking-lutely no reason for you not to be dropshipping. You're leaving thousands upon thousands of dollars on the table. It is a hustle, but it is worth it. I know many of you are slow, so let me make it simple for you.

Dropshipping is a way of selling products online without needing to keep them in stock. When an order is received, the seller sends it to another company who ships the product straight to the customer. The seller is a middleman between the customer and the company with the product.

A dropshipper is a person or business that uses the dropshipping model of buying inventory and fulfillment logistics from a third party, instead of warehousing and shipping the products themselves.

Because dropshipping relies on a third-party supplier to handle inventory warehousing and order fulfillment, a dropshipping operation may be managed by dozens of employees or a single business owner (that's you).

Then you need to choose products to focus on. By focusing on more niche and trending products, you can help get the attention of shoppers and gain traction without competing with larger, established businesses. Niche products often have a more passionate customer base, which can make selling to specific crowds easier by raising awareness for your products.

Fitness, fashion, beauty products, electronics, phone accessories, and yoga-related items may be a good entry point to start dropshipping with no money.

Some examples of a niche dropshipping store could be:
Dog bow ties for dog lovers
iPhone cases for iPhone owners
Camping gear for campers
Exercise equipment for fitness folks

Then you need a supplier. Choosing a dropshipping supplier is a critical step toward creating a successful dropshipping business. Without reliable suppliers, a dropshipping business wouldn't have any products to ship to customers and, therefore, cease to exist.

At this point, you've vetted what dropshipping products you want to sell and know they can be profitable—now you want to make sure you find a dropshipping supplier that gives you the high-quality service you need to grow. Ecommerce platforms like Shopify offer a plug-and-play style option for finding potential suppliers by connecting DSers to your online store.

That's it. Stop jacking off and do the research. Don't overthink. Just do.

THE STOCK MARKET

Anybody with a pair of balls and money in the bank is investing in the stock market. It can be a lucrative venture when approached with careful consideration and a strategic, alpha mindset. While there are inherent risks, anything worth doing is risky.

Understanding the principles of investing can empower you to escape the matrix and harness the potential for financial growth. Here's a guide on how to use investment in the stock market to make money:

Education is Key: Before diving into the stock market, it's essential to equip yourself with a solid understanding of how it works. Learn about stocks, bonds, mutual funds, and other investment vehicles. Familiarize yourself with financial statements, market trends, and the factors influencing stock prices. Various online platforms and educational resources offer valuable insights for both beginners and experienced investors.

Set Clear Financial Goals: Define your financial goals and investment objectives. Are you looking for short-term gains, long-term wealth accumulation, or a balance between the two? Establishing clear goals will guide your investment decisions and help determine your risk tolerance.

Diversification: The age-old adage "don't put all your eggs in one basket" holds true in the stock market. Diversification involves spreading your investments across different sectors, industries, and asset classes to reduce risk. A well-diversified portfolio can provide a buffer against market volatility and minimize the impact of poor-performing assets.

Research and Due Diligence: Informed decisions are the cornerstone of successful investing. Conduct thorough research on companies before investing in their stocks. Analyze financial reports, assess market trends, and stay informed about relevant news that may impact the stock's performance. Tools and resources, such as financial news websites and analysis platforms, can assist in making informed choices.

Long-Term Perspective: While day trading and short-term investments can be tempting, adopting a long-term perspective is often more rewarding. Historically, the stock market has shown an upward trajectory over the long term. Patiently weathering short-term fluctuations can lead to substantial returns over time.

Regular Monitoring and Adjustments: The stock market is dynamic, and economic conditions can change rapidly. Regularly monitor your investments, staying attuned to market trends and company developments. Be prepared to adjust your portfolio based on changing circumstances, and consider rebalancing periodically to align with your financial goals.

Reinvest Dividends: Many companies distribute dividends to shareholders as a share of profits. Reinvesting dividends can accelerate wealth accumulation, as the additional shares purchased through dividends contribute to compounded growth. This approach is particularly effective for long-term investors seeking to capitalize on the power of compounding.

Risk Management: Understanding and managing risk is crucial in stock market investing. Assess your risk tolerance and construct a portfolio that aligns with your comfort level. Consider incorporating risk management tools, such as stop-loss orders, to mitigate potential losses and protect your capital.

Seek Professional Guidance: For those less confident in their investment acumen, seeking advice from financial professionals can be a prudent step. Financial advisors can provide personalized guidance based on your financial goals, risk tolerance, and investment horizon.

Investing in the stock market gives you a pathway to financial freedom. It enables you to harness the power of the matrix without having to buy into the bullshit ideologies. Use the matrix against itself by making money off of it. Take this world by the fucking balls, no apologies.

SEXUAL AND SOCIAL BASICS
BEING DESIRABLE TO WOMEN

Pay attention, losers, because we're about to delve into one of the most crucial aspects of embodying an alpha male who doesn't give a fuck: attracting and maintaining healthy relationships with women.

Now, I understand what you might be thinking: "Andrew, I'm already a charismatic, smooth-talking motherfucker. I don't need any assistance with the fairer kind." Well, let me tell you, dumbass, you're mistaken. If you were as adept with women as you believe, you wouldn't be perusing this book, would you?

First and foremost, if you want to draw in high-quality women, you need to be a high-quality man. That involves taking care of your physique, dressing well, and having your life in order financially. If your life isn't sorted out, why would any woman want to be with you? Get your act together, and the ladies will naturally be drawn to you.

Now, let's discuss confidence. Women can sense insecurity from a mile away, and it's a significant turn-off. Strut into a room as if you own it and make women feel fortunate to be in your presence. If you have to fake it until you make it, do so – eventually, that confidence will become genuine.

In terms of conversation, too many betas mess it up by being dull, predictable, or downright creepy. Don't be that person. Instead, genuinely show interest in what the woman has to say, pose engaging questions, and evoke laughter. Believe me, a good sense of humor is like magic to women. It makes them crave you, and they are attracted to it like moths to a flame.

And for fuck's' sake, avoid being overly needy or clingy. Women despise that behavior. You must have your own life, interests, and friends. If you make a woman the focal point of your world, she'll feel suffocated and lose interest rapidly. That is the epitome of beta behavior.

Now, let's talk about sustaining healthy relationships. This is where many guys falter. They believe that once they've secured a woman, they can coast and stop putting in effort. That's a guaranteed path to ending up alone and discontent, eating ice cream while you jack off alone.

In a relationship, you need to take the lead. This doesn't entail being a controlling jerk – it means assuming responsibility, making decisions, and being a reliable support for your woman when she needs you. It also involves being emotionally accessible and willing to communicate openly and honestly about your emotions. Authentic alpha males aren't afraid to reveal vulnerability.

And don't overlook keeping the romance alive. Surprise your woman with considerate gestures, organize exciting dates, and maintain passion in the bedroom. A robust relationship demands ongoing effort and attention, so resist becoming a complacent bitch.

Finally, let's touch on friendships. A genuine alpha male surrounds himself with other resilient, accomplished men who share his values and aspirations. You are judged by the company you keep, so if you're hanging out with a group of unsuccessful retards, it's time to seek out new friends. Construct a reliable support network of like-minded men who will motivate you to become the best version of yourself.

There you have it, gentlemen. Attracting and nurturing healthy relationships with women isn't rocket science, but it does require exertion, confidence, and a willingness to be open. Step up, assume a leadership role, and witness your love life skyrocket.

BUILDING A NETWORK

Listen up, you lazy fuck. You want to be an alpha male, right? You want to dominate life and excel in all areas, totally and completely? Well, guess what? You're not going to do that by hanging around a bunch of losers who don't have anything going for them.

You need to surround yourself with like-minded men who are just as hungry for success as you are. You might be whining, "But Andrew, how do I find these people?" Don't worry, I've got you covered.

First off, let me tell you a story from my own life. When I started kickboxing, I knew I needed to surround myself with people who were better than me. I sought out training partners who were more skilled and experienced so I could learn from them and become better. If I had just stuck with the same old crowd of douche bags, I would never have become the four-time world champion that I am today.

Let's get back to building your network. It's not as hard as the beta in you thinks it is. You need to do the following:

Eliminate negative influences from your life. If your current associates are hindering your progress, it's time to bid them farewell. Negativity has no place in your journey.

Seek out driven individuals in the right environments. You won't find ambitious, motivated people lounging on their sofas watching Netflix. Attend events, join clubs, and position yourself in scenarios where you're likely to encounter those who align with your aspirations and principles.

Embody the qualities you seek in others. If you desire friendships with successful, motivated individuals, cultivate success and motivation within yourself. Work on personal growth, hone your skills, and evolve into the alpha male you aspire to be. Like-minded individuals will naturally gravitate towards you.

Contribute value. Nobody enjoys the company of a constant taker without giving anything in return. Be someone who provides support, encouragement, and knowledge to your friends. They will value your contributions and likely reciprocate.

Be discerning. A vast network of friends isn't essential. It's preferable to have a smaller, close-knit group of loyal friends than a large circle of acquaintances. Concentrate on nurturing robust connections with a select few who truly matter.

Always bear in mind that you are the average of the five individuals you spend the most time with. Ensure that these individuals contribute positively to your growth. Avoid wasting time on individuals who will drag you down and instead, construct a supportive network of like-minded men. Together, you'll help each other in your transformation from drooling dumbfucks to unstoppable alpha males.

SEDUCTION AND THE FEMALE MIND

APPROACHING AND ATTRACTING WOMEN

You suck with women and you know it. I'm about to drop some serious knowledge on you about the art of approaching and attracting women with confidence. This is some top-level shit that has helped me pull some of the most beautiful women you've ever seen. So grab a pen and paper, and get ready to take notes. Let's clear one thing up: if you're not confident when you approach a woman, you're fucking done. Women can smell insecurity from a mile away, and they're not attracted to that weak beta bullshit. So if you want to be an alpha male, you need to learn how to approach women with confidence. How do you do that? Here are my tried-and-tested tips:

Embrace rejection as an inevitable part of the process. Rejections are bound to happen frequently, but rather than allowing them to shatter your confidence, view each rejection as a valuable learning opportunity. Every instance of rejection presents a chance to refine your approach, so don't shy away from the possibility of failure.

Cultivate comfort in uncomfortable situations. Initiating conversations with women can be intimidating, but it's crucial to confront that fear head-on. The more you engage in such interactions, the more at ease you'll become, and your increasing comfort will project greater confidence.

Maintain an attitude of indifference. Underscored by the principle of caring less about the outcome, adopting an approach that communicates your lack of concern regarding potential rejection can significantly boost your confidence when approaching women.

Prioritize body language. Project confidence through a commanding posture—stand tall, establish eye contact, and assertively own your personal space. A confident physical demeanor not only enhances your appeal to women but also contributes to your own sense of self-assuredness.

Be straightforward and assertive. Avoid ambiguity or overly clever approaches. Instead, confidently approach a woman, introduce yourself, and express your attraction straightforwardly. Women tend to appreciate a man who is clear about his intentions and unafraid to pursue what he desires.

A few years ago, I was at a party in Bucharest. The place was packed with beautiful women, and I had my eye on one bombshell in particular. Instead of hesitating or getting worried about what to say, I walked straight up to her, looked her in the eyes, and said, "I'm Andrew Tate. I saw you from across the room, and I had to come and introduce myself. You are absolutely gorgeous."

She was taken aback by my directness, of course, but She loved it. We spent the rest of the night talking, and I ended up taking her home and fucking her until the early morning. Confidence is the ultimate aphrodisiac, my friends. This woman had been approached by betas who were worried about what to say for years. I was a breath of fresh air, being an alpha male.

If you want to be an alpha male that doesn't give a fuck, you need to learn how to approach and attract women with confidence. Embrace rejection, get comfortable with being uncomfortable, don't give a fuck about the outcome, master your body language, and be direct.

Do these things, and you'll be drowning in ass in no time. Now get out there and start putting this knowledge to work. The world needs more alpha males who aren't afraid to go after what they want. Don't let fear and insecurity hold you back. Be the man you were born to be and start living the life you deserve.

FEMALE PSYCHOLOGY

Alright, you horny losers. Now that you know the basics about how to attract woman, keep reading because I'm about to give you the download on the mysterious world of female psychology. Once you understand how women think, you'll be able to seduce them like a pro. So buckle up and get ready to get your dick wet.

First off, let's not be confused: women are not men. They think differently, they feel differently, and they respond to shit differently. If you want to be successful with women, you need to stop projecting your own male perspective onto them. Now, here's what you need to know about female psychology:

Emotions take precedence. Recognizing that women are inherently emotional beings, it's crucial to understand that they respond more to emotions than logic. Creating a profound emotional connection and evoking positive emotions is a pivotal step in the art of seduction.

Fulfilling the need for validation. Acknowledging a somewhat harsh reality, many women grapple with insecurities and yearn for validation. Making a woman feel desired and appreciated, particularly by portraying her as the most captivating individual in the room, can be a potent strategy.

Unleashing the power of mystery. Women are naturally drawn to men who exude intrigue and maintain an air of mystery. To captivate her interest, resist the temptation to reveal too much about yourself too soon. Allow her to gradually uncover your secrets, keeping her hooked.

The significance of social proof. Women tend to be more attracted to men who enjoy popularity and respect within their social circles. Establishing a robust social network and garnering attention from other women contribute to being perceived as a desirable catch by the woman you're pursuing.

Mastering the push-pull dynamic. Striking a balance between confidence and assertiveness, coupled with the allure of making a woman feel she has earned your attention, is crucial. Creating a dynamic of occasional withdrawal and making her work for your attention will keep her intrigued and engaged.

Now, let me share an anecdote to illustrate the power of understanding female psychology. I was at a club in London, and I spotted a gorgeous woman surrounded by a group of guys. Most men would be intimidated by that situation, but not me. I knew exactly how to use female psychology to my advantage.

I approached the group and immediately focused my attention on her. I asked her about her life and her passions, creating an emotional connection while also validating her. I made her feel like she was the most important person in the room, and the other guys quickly faded into the background.

Throughout the night, I maintained an air of mystery and kept her guessing about my intentions. I also made a point of talking to other women and demonstrating my social proof. Finally, I employed the push-pull dynamic, occasionally withdrawing my attention and making her work to regain it.

By the end of the night, she was hooked. She couldn't resist the psychological cocktail I'd served her, and I ended up taking her home. That, my friends, is the power of understanding female psychology. In conclusion, if you want to be an alpha male that doesn't give a fuck, you need to understand female psychology. Focus on emotions, provide validation, maintain mystery, demonstrate social proof, and use the push-pull dynamic. Once you master these principles, you'll have women lining up to be with you.

Now go out there and put this knowledge to the test. Remember, the world needs more alpha males who know how to handle women. Don't let your own ignorance hold you back. Understand female psychology, and become the man that every woman wants.

KNOWLEDGE AND SKILL SET
SELF-IMPROVE CONSTANTLY

Pay attention, you inadequate fucking bores. Still yearning to transform into a genuine alpha male? Well, listen up – it's not an instantaneous process. You need to consistently invest in yourself, acquire new knowledge, and never reach a point where you're content. That's the only path to evolving into the type of man worthy of the good life.

I've witnessed countless failures who believe they've achieved success just because they have a decent job, a partner, or some money in the bank. Let me enlighten you – that's insufficient. If you genuinely aspire to be an alpha male, you must persistently challenge yourself, perpetually enhance your skills, and refuse to settle for anything less than excellence.

Here's how you can commence your journey of perpetual self-improvement:

Cultivate a mindset focused on growth. Firmly believe that there is always room for improvement, regardless of your current level of expertise. Whether you're already excelling or not, maintaining the mentality that progress is constant is crucial.

Establish clear goals. Don't merely fantasize about the person you desire to become. Outline specific, measurable objectives and dedicate yourself to their pursuit each day. Upon achieving those goals, set new ones immediately. Embrace an unending commitment to personal advancement.

Seek knowledge from the best. Becoming a four-time world kickboxing champion wasn't achieved by watching random YouTube videos. Instead, I sought out top-tier trainers and fighters to learn from their expertise. Identify individuals who have already mastered their craft, whether in business, sports, or any other field, and absorb their knowledge.

Maintain curiosity. The world is filled with intriguing aspects, and there's always more to discover. Refrain from complacency and assuming you know everything. Foster curiosity, ask questions, and consistently expand your understanding.

Challenge your limits persistently. Without testing your capabilities, you'll never uncover your true potential. Dare to push your boundaries, continually challenge yourself, and take calculated risks. This is the sole path to genuine personal growth.

You might be wondering, "Andrew, how do you, a genius, find time for self-improvement?" Here's the secret – I make time. Prioritizing self-improvement takes precedence over indulging in stupid, jerk-off activities like watching TV or playing video games. I allocate my time to reading, training, and enhancing my businesses.

Therefore, if your aspiration is to embody the alpha male who doesn't give a fuck, it's imperative to take your self-improvement seriously. Distance yourself from those content with mediocrity and surround yourself with individuals committed to growth and success.

Never settle for your current state – the responsibility lies with you to carve out a meaningful existence. Embrace continuous self-improvement, get moving, and evolve into the alpha male you were destined to be.

LEARN FROM THE SUCCESS OF OTHERS

You know what's the difference between an alpha male and a broke beta bitch? The alpha male learns from the success of others, while the broke loser sits around feeling sorry for himself, blaming everyone else for his failures. If you want to be an alpha male, you need to start learning from the success of others. Listen up, because I'm about to share some hard-hitting truths that will transform your life if you have the balls to apply them. First things first, you've got to stop being a hater. I've seen so many idiots who spend their time hating on successful people, instead of learning from them. These are the same mouthbreathers who claim that successful people are "lucky" or that they "cheated" their way to the top.

Newsflash, you fuckwad: Success doesn't come from luck or cheating. It comes from hard work, discipline, and learning from the people who've already made it. So, how do you learn from the success of others? Here's a step-by-step guide:

Seek out role models who have achieved success in your chosen field or area of interest, regardless of whether they are billionaires, athletes, or accomplished artists. Identify individuals who have attained the level of success you aspire to reach.

Examine their life stories by delving into their biographies, watching interviews, and gaining comprehensive insights into their paths to success. Understand the habits, mindsets, and strategies that contributed to their achievements.

Replicate their success by adopting the habits, mindsets, and strategies that proved effective for your chosen role models. If they adhere to a 5 am wake-up routine, follow suit. If they prioritize reading a book weekly, incorporate that into your routine. Mirror their dedication to spending two hours daily honing their craft by dedicating a similar amount of time to your pursuits.

Establish connections with successful individuals, recognizing the transformative impact of surrounding yourself with accomplished peers. Attend conferences, join clubs, and take any necessary steps to immerse yourself in environments where you can interact with those you admire.

Draw valuable lessons from their failures, recognizing that understanding their mistakes is as crucial as emulating their successes. Identify the errors they made and strive to avoid repeating them.

Allow me to share a personal anecdote. When embarking on my journey to become a world-class kickboxer, I didn't casually stroll into a gym and start punching bags. Instead, I actively sought out the best trainers and fighters available, learning extensively from their expertise. This encompassed studying their techniques, training methods, and mindset. The outcome? I achieved the status of a four-time world kickboxing champion.

This principle extends to every facet of your life. If aspiring to be a successful entrepreneur, glean insights from the most accomplished business minds. If aiming for a remarkable physique, draw inspiration from elite fitness trainers and bodybuilders. Abandon the know-it-all mentality and embrace the opportunity to learn from those who have truly realized what you aspire to achieve.

In essence, to embody the alpha male who doesn't give a damn, commence a journey of learning from the successes of others. This rapid assimilation of knowledge is the key to elevating your life and evolving into the type of man universally admired and respected. Remember: the only obstacle in your path is yourself. Step aside, clear the way, and begin learning from the very best.

SURROUND YOURSELF WITH SUCCESS
NETWORKING AND HOBBIES

If you want to be a true alpha male, you need to surround yourself with successful people and fill your life with hobbies that you're genuinely passionate about. No one wants to be friends with a loser who spends his days jerking off and playing video games. It's time to level up your social life and find some shit that makes you excited to wake up in the morning.

First, let's talk about networking with successful people. You know that old saying, "You are the average of the five people you spend the most time with"? Well, it's fucking true. If you hang around a bunch of broke, miserable losers, you'll end up becoming one too. So ditch the dead weightand start connecting with people who are actually going somewhere in life.

Here are some tips on networking like a boss:

Attend various events and conferences. Break free from your comfort zone and actively participate in gatherings where accomplished individuals converge. This might involve industry conferences, networking functions, or upscale venues like exclusive clubs and bars. The key is to position yourself where you can connect with the caliber of people you aspire to engage with.

Cultivate genuine interest in others. When encountering

new individuals, prioritize understanding their stories and experiences. Pose thoughtful questions, actively listen to their narratives, and demonstrate authentic curiosity about their lives. People appreciate being heard, and making them feel acknowledged increases the likelihood of being remembered.

Contribute value. Avoid the pitfall of being a mere recipient and focus on providing value to those you encounter. Whether it's sharing your expertise, facilitating connections, or simply being a supportive companion, finding ways to enhance the experiences of those around you will make you a sought-after presence. The more value you bring to interactions, the more people will be drawn to your company.

Then you need fulfilling hobbies, shit to get you out of your bedroom and into the world. If all you do is work, eat, sleep, repeat every day, you will burn out fast. You'll need to ditch your boring-ass ways and find constructive hobbies that round you out as a full, robust individual.

Below are some tips on finding hobbies you are passionate about:

Experiment with different activities. You won't know if you enjoy something until you try it. So go out and try a bunch of different shit – join a sports team, take a cooking class, learn a musical instrument, or start painting. You never know what might ignite your passion.

Don't be afraid to fail. Not every hobby you try will be a home run, and that's okay. The point is to find something that you enjoy and can become skilled at over time. So don't worry if you suck at first – embrace the learning process and keep pushing forward.

Make it social. Hobbies are more fun when you share them with others. Join clubs or groups related to your interests, and you'll not only improve your skills but also expand your social circle.

So there you have it. If you want to be an alpha male who doesn't give a fuck, you need to network with successful people and find hobbies that make you happy. Start attending events, being genuinely interested in others, and offering value. Experiment with different activities, embrace failure, and make your hobbies social. Remember, life is too short to be a broke, boring loser. Surround yourself with success, fill your life with passion, and watch as your alpha male status skyrockets. Now get the fuck out there and start living your best life.

THE BENEFITS OF CONNECTION

If you think being an alpha male is all about being jacked and banging chicks, you've got it all wrong. Sure, those things are important, but if you really want to be the ultimate alpha male, you need to build a powerful social circle and have diverse interests.

Let me break it down for you – here's why it's crucial to be well-connected and have a wide range of hobbies. Being well-connected means you have access to opportunities and resources that the average Joe doesn't. When you know the right people, doors open up for you.

Think about it – if you're friends with the CEO of a company, it's a hell of a lot easier to land that high-paying job than if you're just some nobody off the street. So stop being a lazy fuck and start networking like your life depends on it. Not only will your connections help you in your career, but they can also improve your personal life.

Imagine having friends who can get you into exclusive parties or hook you up with discounts at their businesses. When you're well-connected, your life becomes exponentially more enjoyable.

Now let's talk about having diverse interests. If all you do is sit at home and jerk off to porn, you're a boring motherfucker. Nobody wants to be around someone who has nothing interesting to say. By having a variety of hobbies, you become a more well-rounded and intriguing person.

Plus, having diverse interests can also benefit your mental health. Studies have shown that people who engage in a wide range of activities are generally happier and less stressed than those who don't. So, not only will you be more interesting to others, but you'll also feel better about yourself. Here are some of the key benefits of being well-connected and having diverse interests:

Expanded opportunities: Associating with influential individuals opens doors to job prospects, business ventures, and various opportunities that can significantly enhance your overall success and status.

Enriched social life: A robust social circle ensures a constant array of companions, whether it's for a vibrant night out or a relaxed barbecue gathering at a friend's place.

Stimulating conversations: Possessing diverse interests provides a continuous source of engaging topics, transforming you into an intriguing conversationalist and attracting people to interact with you effortlessly.

Personal development: Exploring a range of hobbies pushes you beyond your comfort zone, encouraging the acquisition of new skills and fostering a well-rounded and adaptable personality.

Enhanced mental well-being: Involvement in various activities contributes to stress reduction, heightened happiness, and an increased sense of fulfillment in life.

Now that you understand the benefits, it's time to get off your lazy ass and start building connections and exploring new interests. Attend networking events, join clubs, and try out different hobbies.

Remember, if you want to be an alpha male who doesn't give a fuck, you need to create a powerful social circle and have diverse interests. So get out there and start living a life that others can only dream of. Embrace your inner alpha, and watch as your life becomes more exciting, fulfilling, and more soaked in pussy juice.

NEVER STOP IMPROVING

Alright, motherfuckers, this is it – the final chapter. If you've made it this far, then congrats, you're not a complete pussy. But guess what? The journey doesn't end here.

Being an alpha male who doesn't give a fuck is a lifelong pursuit of self-improvement. You don't just hit a certain level and then coast for the rest of your life. Nah, fuck that. You've got to keep pushing yourself, keep learning, and keep growing. That's what it's all about.

Listen, life is a never-ending game, and if you ain't playing to win, you're just wasting your fucking time. Embracing self-improvement means constantly seeking new ways to grow, evolve, and dominate. It means learning from your failures, not dwelling on them like some pussy-ass brookie.

You think I, TopG, got to where I am today by being complacent? Fuck no. I've faced countless obstacles and setbacks, but I didn't let them break me. I took those experiences and used them to build an empire. I've won world championships, made millions, and traveled the world – all because I refused to accept mediocrity.

So, how do you embrace the lifelong pursuit of self-improvement? Here are some key steps to get you started:

Never stop learning: Keep reading books (only the great ones, otherwise skip reading), attending seminars, and learning from others and getting shit done. The more you know, the more powerful you become. Knowledge is fucking power, my friends.

Set goals and crush them: Always have a target in mind – something to strive for. Whether it's a new business venture, a fitness goal, or learning a new skill, set a goal and then demolish it. Remember, you're an alpha male who doesn't give a fuck, so act like it.

Surround yourself with winners: You're the average of the five people you spend the most time with. So make sure you're hanging out with successful, motivated motherfuckers who are on the same path as you. Losers will only drag you down.

Embrace failure: Failure is inevitable, but it's how you handle it that matters. When you fuck up, don't wallow in self-pity. Instead, learn from it and come back stronger. Use failure as fuel to propel you forward.

Keep pushing your limits: Don't get comfortable. Comfort is the enemy of progress. Always seek new challenges and push yourself to be better than you were yesterday. That's how you become a true alpha male.

Remember, you're building a legacy. When you're on your deathbed, do you want to look back on a life of mediocrity and regret? Or do you want to know that you lived like a fucking king, conquering every challenge that came your way? I know what I had to choose.

You see, the matrix dealt me a vicious hand that forced me down a dark path that I didn't deserve. That path ended in incarceration. But strangely, that seemingly desolate period of my life, a period where freedom was a distant memory, became the crucible that forged me even further into a man of resilience, determination, and an undeniable alpha mindset.

It would have been easy to give up, but that isn't the Andrew Tate way. The first lesson prison taught me was resilience. It was a sink-or-swim scenario where only the resilient survived. The harsh realities of prison life demanded toughness, both physically and mentally. The constant threat of violence, the rigid routines, and the isolation – they all contributed to me fully realizing that my method of living was not only beneficial but totally necessary for survival.

In a place where vulnerability was a liability, I learned to cloak my emotions. Every hardship, every indignity, became a stepping stone to my transformation. The thick skin I developed wasn't just a shield; it was a symbol of my metamorphosis into a man who could weather any storm, emerging unbroken on the other side.

Inside the confined space, where freedom was a distant dream, I discovered the true value of hard work and grit. The monotonous routine of prison life forced me to find purpose in the mundane. I embraced work details with an unwavering determination, whether it was scrubbing floors, folding laundry, or toiling in the prison yard under the unforgiving sun.

As I engaged in these menial tasks, a sense of pride welled within me. It wasn't about the work itself; it was about proving to myself that I could rise above my circumstances. In that confined space, where opportunities were scarce, I cultivated a work ethic that would become the foundation of my future success.

The barred windows and concrete walls became a constant reminder of the freedom I had lost. Freedom, once taken for granted, now held unparalleled value. The taste of it lingered in the crisp air that seeped through the tiny cell window. Every day spent within those confines fueled my longing for the open sky, for the wind on my face, for the unrestricted horizon.

It was in the deprivation of freedom that I learned its true significance. The simple act of walking down the street, feeling the ground beneath my feet, became a cherished vision. Each day in captivity etched a profound appreciation for liberty into my consciousness. I promised myself that if I ever regained that freedom, I would seize it with both hands and never let go.

Emerging from the shadows of prison, I carried with me the lessons learned and the strength gained. The hardships, the toil, and the yearning for freedom had crafted a version of myself that was unyielding, resilient, and driven by an unwavering sense of purpose.

My journey from bars to breakthrough had instilled in me the essence of an alpha male. No longer defined by the mistakes of my past, I stood tall, unapologetic for the scars that adorned my soul. The hardships, the relentless work, and the longing for freedom had not broken me; they had molded me into a force to be reckoned with.

True alpha status isn't about dominating others; it's about mastering oneself. It's about facing adversity head-on, embracing the grind, and appreciating the freedom that so many take for granted. Every step taken in the free world became a testament to my resilience, a celebration of my hard work, and a declaration of my unwavering freedom.

In the grand tapestry of my life, the chapter spent behind bars wasn't a period of defeat; it was a transformative crucible that ignited the flames of my alpha spirit. As I walked away from the prison gates, I carried within me the indomitable spirit of one who had faced darkness and emerged into the light – a true alpha male, empowered by the journey from confinement to unbridled freedom.

If I could do it, you can too. I doubt you're dealing with the circumstances I was dealing with, so you have no excuse. Take back your freedom from the matrix and forge a path, taking your destiny by the reigns.

So, my fellow alphas, it's time to embark on the never-ending journey of self-improvement. Keep pushing, keep striving, and never settle for anything less than greatness. This is your life, so make it fucking legendary. Now go forth and be the alpha male that doesn't give a fuck. Your empire awaits.

Printed in Great Britain
by Amazon

36662789R00040